BEST DRESSED SOUTHERN SALADS

BEST DRESSED
SOUTHERN SALADS

FROM KEY WEST TO WASHINGTON, D.C.

Vicky Moon

A Capital Lifestyles Book

CAPITAL
BOOKS, INC.
Sterling, Virginia

Capital Books, Inc.
P.O. Box 605
Herndon, Virginia 20172-0605

Library of Congress Cataloging-in-Publication Data
Moon, Vicky.
Best dressed southern salads : from Key West to Washington, D.C. / Vicky Moon.
p.   cm.
ISBN 1-892123-81-9
1. Salads.   2. Cookery, American Southern style.   I. Title.
TX807 .M66   2002
641.8′3′0975 dc21   2002067384

Printed in Canada on acid-free paper that meets the
American National Standards Institute Z39-48 Standard.

First Edition

10 9 8 7 6 5 4 3 2 1

In memory of Laurie Gilbert Stewart
(a charter member of GRITS: Girls Raised in the South)
and much thanks to
Claudia Young

Washington, D.C.

Richmond

Raleigh

Greenville

Atlanta

Charleston

Ocala

Palm Beach

Key West

© Big Truck Maps

CONTENTS

INTRODUCTION

$\mathcal{I}$ have driven between Florida and Washington, D.C. more times than I wish to count. As a little girl I remember my parents would often go out of the way to stop at Aunt Fanny's Cabin in Smyrna, Georgia. I came across one of its old postcards while I was putting this book together. "Real Southern Food Near Atlanta," it says. "Save your Confederate money folks, the South will rise again." I looked up Aunt Fanny's on the Internet; the place has been dismantled, but you can stop in Smyrna at the visitor's center and see all kinds of Aunt Fanny memorabilia.

For this book, I am taking a literary road trip from Key West to Washington, D.C. (sort of from Margaritaville to Egoville). I'm stopping along the way at favorite places, to visit friends. I've named some of the recipes after streets in cities like Palm Beach, Atlanta, and Raleigh. I'm passing along the names of a few good places to eat, although in my mind, nothing will ever quite match Aunt Fanny's.

My college roommate made me swear I wouldn't divulge her name when I wrote what she told me about her take on Southern salads versus Northern salads. She was busy on this early afternoon, moving her winter clothes to the attic and getting out spring cottons and linens. The painter was there, her husband was out turkey hunting, and she felt "fatigued." Still, she had a moment for a chat. She speaks slowly with a delightful (yet thick) accent, which could prompt some to request an interpreter in order to grasp what she's saying. On this day, she didn't even have to pause to consider—it came right out. Simple. And I don't want to cause another "War between the States" but . . . "The Yanks don't care as long as it's green and it crunches."

Okay, at first glance it may not seem that there's a difference in something like a salad in New York and one in Palm Beach. Sure, Caesar salads in all restaurants are similar. But for our purposes here, we're talking about homemade salads. Salads for the garden club luncheon, salads for a classic dinner party for eight or a brunch by the pool. At-home food, not store bought. Nobody in America can deny such a thing as regional food, can she?

Whenever I inquired about Southern salads, one word kept popping up over and over . . . *congealed*. "As a child I remember congealed salads—Bing Cherry—but don't see them much anymore," says Gwen Spann from Charlotte. "I would say a southern salad would be congealed," says Jane Carlson from Richmond.

Louise Sinclaire of Washington, D.C. is not only an authority on food but has also taught cooking. She tells the story about overhearing the conversation of two locals when she was in the ladies room of a hotel in Charleston. "The subject was a luncheon menu," she says. "One woman was not sure the banquet department understood what an important do this was going to be. The other asked what she thought was missing? The reply was: 'There's no congealed salad.' "

So let's just get this out of the way right now. I'm not going to offer twenty-two different congealed salads, which basically is gelatin with fruit. But I will offer one. I have dedicated this book to my late great friend Laurie Gilbert Stewart. A Southern sparkler through and through, she loved salads. Her husband sent this via e-mail:

Ginger Ale Fruit Salad

1 large (6 ounce) package lemon gelatin	1 (no. 2) can fruit cocktail
1/2 cup hot water	1½ cups ginger ale
	1/2 cup chopped pecans

Dissolve gelatin in hot water. Add fruit cocktail (without juice), ginger ale, and pecans to gelatin. Pour into mold. A dash of ginger adds to flavor. Serves 5.

The other word that continually surfaces in the South is ... *mayonnaise.* It almost qualifies as a food group. Again, Jane Carlson relates, "One wag I know referred to mayonnaise as the 'official condiment of Virginia.'" Jane's sister sent me an e-mail: "I know the book is done, but I was at luncheon in Richmond yesterday, where we had chicken salad (with mayo), shrimp salad (with mayo), aspic, and two kinds of extra mayo. Ham biscuits and key lime pie. Jane said she expected me to run out in front and call you on my cell." Food group or condiment, I offer here nine variations of mayo. (If you have cholesterol concerns, forget it.)

Don't get the impression that I'm just talking about Jello and mayo, fried chicken, and cole slaw. (Referred to simply as "slaw." Because ... when it comes down to it, Southern cooks can be imaginative, inspired, and inventive.)

And, finally, there's a Southern legend about the traditional stereotypical little woman. She should be a gracious hostess in the parlor, a fabulous cook in the kitchen, and dynamite in the bedroom. (Like I said . . . imaginative, inspired, and inventive.)

But most important of all? They never get caught "undressed."

Chapter 1

THE SUNSHINE STATE

Florida is where I grew up, so I know it well. Here are some of my favorite recipes from some of my favorite places. You'll find that the recipes throughout this book are named for my favorite streets in each town. That's not necessarily because they come from that particular street, but because many of these recipes are generic Southern of the area (spiced up by me or my friends, of course) and needed a more exciting name. They also help you picture the drive up the coast you'll take with me on this Southern road trip and eating adventure.

Key West

We begin at mile marker number one, Key West, Florida—also known as The Conch Republic. While we know that Southern food is distinctive, the cuisine here must be separated from the rest of Florida. It has a touch of the Caribbean with a dash of Cuba and a hint of Spain. It's foreign and fun. These are the things that come to mind:

Conch . . . in every form. As Forrest Gump might say, "There's conch chowder, conch fritters, and (of course) conch salad."

Key limes. Limeade . . . whenever I visit, I stop downtown on the last morning and buy a large limeade to take on the long drive north from Key West. (My friend Doc Saffer would say, "Limeade just doesn't taste right without Vodka." But, you be the judge.)

Chickens. They're everywhere and known as Wild Gypsy Chickens. At one time the pastime of cockfighting was very popular down here. (And really, who's to say it doesn't still go on?) But for now they're (almost) sacred. In the colorful area of Key West called The Bahamian Village, they roam among the guests at one of my very favorite restaurants, Blue Heaven (www.blueheavenkw.com). And there's now a store called The Chicken Store (what else?) where "the roosters are stars." The store serves as a refuge for wounded, orphaned, and sick chickens. They are available for adoption if you qualify. Do not mention the words *potpie* or *chicken salad* here (www.thechickenstore.com).

The etymology of Key West comes from Cayo Hueso, or Bone Key, said to be the icon of the bones of the first inhabitants. Native American Indians such as the Calusas, Tequestas, and the Matecumbes originally inhabited the four- by two-mile island. Spanish explorers, led by Ponce de León, landed here in 1513. In 1908, Henry Morrison Flagler started his famous East Coast Railroad (know as Flagler's Folly) to connect Key West with the mainland. It took twenty years to complete. Driving south from Miami, the ruins of the railroad can be seen from along U.S. 1, as the aquatic shades of bottle green, turquoise, and deep azure stretch out on both sides. (See also Palm Beach!)

These are the things to do and see in Key West: watch the sunset from Mallory Square; go shopping on Duvall Street (the locals complain that it's full of T-shirt shops but it's amusing to at least read them—they're filthy and fun); visit the Audubon House and Gardens; and take a tour of the circa 1890 two-story white frame house called Truman's Little White House, where President Harry Truman spent 175 days during office. (Hint: For a special treat, there's a private two-bedroom suite with porch and sundeck available to rent.) And take a ride on the Conch Train, tourist like—yes, we *are* tourists—it's informative and relaxing.

Key West has always been known as a writer's retreat. During the winter there are conferences and discussion groups, such as The Key West Literary Seminar. I once attended one led by Mary Lee Settle. She was a taskmaster and demanding—not to the writers but to the folks sponsoring the group. She didn't like the Xerox machine, she didn't like the coffee, she didn't like her accommodations, and so on. But despite her idiosyncrasies the rest of us loved the seminar. We met each morning in a delightful old wooden building, where we would have coffee and go over our work.

And then, there's the must see on every writer's list . . . The Hemingway House. Now occupied by descendants of his six-toed cats (known as polydactyl), I visit the home every time I'm in Key West. While standing in his dining room or writing nook one can "feel" old Key West. Finally, with a peek inside Hemingway's favorite watering hole, Sloppy Joe's Bar, a few "Papa" look-a-likes might be spotted.

Here are my favorite recipes.

Conch Salad
(To Beat Them All)

This salad is best served with Bimini bread, which has a light sweet taste and is a specialty of the area.

Juice of six Key limes
Juice of two oranges
3 medium pieces conch
1 cup diced red onion
1 green bell pepper, diced

2 tablespoons diced red bell pepper
2 cucumbers, diced
1/2 teaspoon of Tabasco or other
   hot sauce

Tenderize conch with large wooden mallet. (This is very important so it will not be tough.) Beat the hell out of it! Then cut up conch into small bite-size pieces and place in bowl. Add Key lime and orange juice and marinate overnight. Combine remaining ingredients in glass bowl and add hot sauce. Chill for several hours. Before serving, add conch and toss.

Duvall Street

This is a very old and popular bacon dressing to be poured over endive or iceberg, a traditional salad. It would be good served with meatloaf (that's right, meatloaf) a popular dinner entrée in Key West.

4 slices bacon
1/2 cup sugar
1/2 teaspoon salt
1 egg, beaten

1/4 cup vinegar
1 cup water
Salt to taste
Sugar to taste

Fry bacon slowly; crumble very fine and reserve fat. In saucepan mix sugar and salt. Stir in egg and vinegar; add water, bacon, and fat. Cook to desired thickness. Add salt and sugar. Makes $1\frac{1}{2}$ cups.

Simonton Street

1 tablespoon sweet sake (rice wine)
  or dry sherry
2 tablespoons rice wine
  vinegar
1 tablespoon sugar
1 tablespoon soy sauce

1/2 large daikon or white radish, cut
  into matchstick pieces *or* about
  9 ounces red radishes, cut into
  matchstick pieces to
  equal 1 cup
1 large carrot, cut into matchstick
  pieces to equal 1 cup

Combine sake, vinegar, sugar, and soy sauce in bowl. Add radish and carrot; toss to mix. Marinate covered in refrigerator for at least 1 hour. Make $1\frac{1}{2}$ cups.

Caroline Street

8 ounces blue cheese, crumbled
16 ounces sour cream
1 tablespoon mayonnaise

1 clove garlic, minced
Dash Worcestershire sauce
Dash white pepper

Blend ingredients with fork. This can be thinned with milk, if desired. Chill. Makes 3 cups.

Southernmost Salad

Serve with endive, celery, ham, and apples. And, when in Key West, try with the Pain au Levain, a French country sourdough bread from Cole's Peace Artisan Bakery at the corner of Eaton and Grinnell. In December 1997, Kurt Matarazzo opened the bakery, located in a historic, rustic wooden house, once a Cuban grocery store. It's a good place to stop for a coffee and croissant after a morning walk around the island. The bakery uses whole grains, untreated flour, and live leavening cultures to create breads such as onion dill, mango boules, and ciabitta. Visit its Web site at www.colespeace.com.

1/2 cup sugar	1/4 cup water
1/2 cup catsup	1 teaspoon salt
1/2 cup salad oil	1 small grated onion
1/4 cup cider vinegar	1/4 teaspoon mixed salad herbs

Combine all ingredients in jar with lid and shake well. Makes 1 pint.

Green Street

Serve on spinach salad topped with blackened red snapper.

3/4 cup red wine vinegar
3/4 cup chili sauce
1 cup salad oil

1 tablespoon soy sauce
1/2 cup sugar
Salt to taste

Mix all ingredients. Add crumbled bacon, chopped hard-boiled eggs, and red onions, to taste. Makes $2\frac{1}{2}$ cups.

South Beach

Moving up the coast to the Miami area, we stop only briefly in South Beach. Here, I present a surprising blend of brown sugar, celery seed, and dry mustard with red wine vinegar and olive oil. Serve it over Bibb lettuce, Florida oranges, Florida avocados, and sliced tomatoes (from Florida, of course). It's best nibbled while watching the world go by in one of the liveliest neighborhoods imaginable (you'll remember South Beach from the movie *The Birdcage*, and you might also want to read anything written by Carl Hiaasen and Edna Buchanan).

1/2 cup brown sugar
1 teaspoon salt
1 teaspoon dry mustard
1 teaspoon celery seed

1 teaspoon paprika
4 tablespoons red wine vinegar
3/4 cup salad oil

Mix together by vigorously stirring with wire whisk and pour over salad immediately. Makes 1 cup.

Fort Lauderdale

One hundred and eighty-seven miles north of Key West, Fort Lauderdale is known as "The Venice of America." It found a place on the national map in the 1960s with the movie *Where the Boys Are*, starring the perpetually tan George Hamilton. A circa 1901 trading post owned by Frank Stranahan along the New River still stands as the oldest building.

Things to do: Head to Las Olas, a boulevard of boutiques and restaurants (personal favorite—Café de Paris), for a day of shopping and a nice lunch; visit Butterfly World; or take a ride on the Jungle Queen (you can still see the Seminole Indians wrestle an alligator). Hit the races at Calder Race Track, or for funky stuff and the knockoff Rolex watches and Gucci handbags, there are two fabulous flea markets: The Festival Flea Market on Sample Road and The Swap Shop on Sunrise Boulevard. The Baltimore Orioles claim Fort Lauderdale as their winter home, and years ago the New York Yankees had spring training here. The Yankee Clipper Hotel along A1A on the beach was named in honor of the late Joe DiMaggio.

It's Mecca for yacht lovers; sleek ninety and one hundred–foot–plus vessels glide up and down the Intracoastal Waterway past landmarks such as Pier 66 and Bahia Mar (made famous by the late writer John D. MacDonald and his fictional character Travis McGee). The big boats sometimes stop for lunch or dinner at the Lauderdale Yacht Club or the Coral Ridge Yacht Club. Parties are planned well in advance for the highlight of the year in early December . . . the Boat Parade.

Sunrise Boulevard

The locals flock to lunch at a certain major department store in the Galleria Mall on Sunrise Boulevard. The fresh fruit with poppy seed dressing is a favorite with the ladies. This Dallas-based store does not allow the recipe to be given out, but after many years and many lunches it was slipped over the counter to me one day.

$1\frac{1}{2}$ cups sugar	2/3 cup apple cider vinegar
2 teaspoons dry mustard	2 cups vegetable oil
1 teaspoon salt	3 tablespoons poppy seeds

Combine sugar, mustard, salt, and vinegar in blender. Slowly add oil, blending until very thick. Stir in poppy seeds. Keep in airtight container in refrigerator. Will last about 2 to 3 weeks. Makes $4\frac{1}{4}$ cups.

Harbor Beach Honey Celery Seed

1/2 cup sugar
1 teaspoon dry mustard
1 teaspoon paprika
1 teaspoon celery seed
$1\frac{1}{4}$ teaspoons salt

1 teaspoon grated onion
1/3 cup honey
1 tablespoon lemon juice
1 cup salad oil
1/3 cup orange/mint vinegar

Combine dry ingredients. Add onion, honey, and lemon juice. Beat in electric mixer or with rotary beater. Add oil very slowly, beating constantly to make an emulsion. Add orange/mint vinegar as mixture becomes thick. Continue to beat a few minutes after last of oil is added. Chill. Will keep in refrigerator for several months. Orange-mint vinegar enhances flavor. Makes $2\frac{1}{2}$ cups.

Orange-Mint Vinegar

3 oranges, thinly peeled	Vinegar, 5 percent white
2 cups fresh mint	

Peel oranges, removing all white membrane. Wash mint and shake dry. Place peel (sliced) and mint in 1-quart jar and fill with 5 percent vinegar. Cap and store for several weeks—at least 4 or 5. Filter into container and cap again. Do not strain. Use chemically pure filter paper.

Las Olas Boulevard
Club Salad Dressing for Pasta

This is best with a pasta salad of chicken, bacon, and sweet red peppers.

3/4 cup Thousand Island Dressing
1 tablespoon chopped onion
1 hard-boiled egg, chopped
1 teaspoon Worcestershire sauce

1/8 teaspoon Tabasco sauce
Salt and pepper to taste
Parsley flakes

Blend together and chill. Makes 1 cup.

Victoria Park Old-Fashioned Dressing

Named for one of the oldest and most charming neighborhoods in Fort Lauderdale—Victoria Park—it's perfect for cole slaw.

---

1 can Eagle Brand Condensed Milk
1 teaspoon salt

1/2 cup vinegar
1 teaspoon dry mustard

Blend together. Makes $1\frac{3}{4}$ cups.

Galt Ocean Mile

Arthur T. Galt traveled south to Florida from Chicago in the early 1920s and bought eight thousand acres of land along the Intracoastal Waterway to develop. This area of Fort Lauderdale is now lined with luxury condos along the beach.

---

1 can Eagle Brand Condensed Milk
$1\frac{1}{2}$ teaspoons mustard

1 teaspoon paprika
1 cup sour cream

Blend together. Makes 3 cups.

Coral Ridge Horseradish Cream

Serve on romaine lettuce with hot steak accompanied by a full-bodied red wine. Also great with beef or pork alone.

1/4 cup heavy cream, whipped
1 or 2 tablespoons prepared
  horseradish

1/4 teaspoon salt
1/8 teaspoon paprika

Whip cream. Combine horseradish, salt, and paprika and then fold into whipped cream. Makes 1/2 cup.

Nurmi Isles Fruit Dressing

This is good with all types of fruit: bananas, peaches, melons, grapes, pineapple. Or with any type of berries. How can one not think of a fruit salad in Florida? This vintage recipe is in honor of Victor Nurmi. Originally from Finland, he developed four "isles" off Las Olas Boulevard in 1944–46. He had more than fifty workers build bridges, seawalls, and streets, one of which is named for him.

1/4 cup vinegar
1/4 cup milk
3/4 cup sugar
1 teaspoon salt
1 teaspoon dry mustard

1/8 teaspoon white pepper
2 eggs, beaten
1 dozen large marshmallows
1 cup whipping cream, beaten until
   stiff

Combine all ingredients except marshmallows and whipped cream in medium saucepan. Stir mixture over medium heat until it boils and becomes thick. Add marshmallows and stir until melted. Let stand until cool. Fold in whipped cream. Makes $2\frac{1}{2}$ cups.

Palm Beach

Palm Beach, forty-five miles north, is the winter playground of the rich and famous. It was put on the map in the late nineteenth century by Henry Morrison Flagler, a cofounder of Standard Oil.

Flagler built his famous East Coast Railroad from the northeast with a stop in what was once a swamp, where he had also assembled two magnificent resorts: The Breakers and the Royal Poinciana Hotel. At the age of seventy-one he built his winter home, Whitehall, for his thirty-four-year-old wife, Mary Lily Kenan. It has been referred to as an American version of Buckingham Palace or even the Taj Mahal. Completed in 1902, the sixty thousand–square–foot house had fifty-five rooms. Now known as the Flagler Museum, it has been meticulously restored and is the setting for many charity and social events.

The buildings and the beaches in Palm Beach are glaringly white. Large, dark sunglasses (à la Jackie Kennedy) are in order. Pack your lime green and shocking pink Lily Pulitzer pants and a cable knit cashmere sweater to wear over your shoulders at night. Men should leave their socks at home; women should buy a pair of classic Palm Beach sandals (again à la Jackie) from the workrooms of Stephen Bonanno.

The Mediterranean-inspired architecture of Addison Mizner featuring terracotta barrel roof tiles, secluded courtyards, textured stucco, and Moorish arcades is revered in Palm Beach. Other inspirational architects of times gone by are John Volk and Maurice Fatio.

The locals eat breakfast at Green's Pharmacy and lunch at Hamburger Heaven (both very informal). I was having lunch at Hamburger Heaven one day, sitting with my back against the wall as I always do, so I can watch what's coming and going. I was with my dear cousin Bonnie from Phoenix and I said to her, "Oh, there's Ethel." And she replied, "Ethel who?" How could I be too intolerant? She's my cousin. But need you ask? This has always been a Kennedy hot spot (sometimes too hot, but we don't want to get too far into that, do we?).

The Bath and Tennis Club and the Everglades Club are members only, so try the Colony Bar or the Leopard Lounge at the Chesterfield Hotel. The Taboo Restaurant has been the site for many a rendezvous through the years, and other places of note include Bici, Café L'Europe, and Renato's.

For the ultimate in recreation take a walk up and down Worth Avenue, providing a splendid afternoon of retail extravagance. Be sure to hit Stubbs & Wootton, Chris Kellog, A Perfect Day in Paradise, Johnny Brown's, and two of my very favorites...The Brighton Pavilion and Devonshire.

Nelson Hammel and business partner Pete Hawkins started an English garden shop called Devonshire in Middleburg, Virginia, in 1982. The shop features massive stone ornaments and large elegant containers along with a collection of garden accoutrements. Since then, it has grown to eleven shops around the country (Carmel, Westport, Naples, Nantucket, New York, Bridgehampton, Newport, and Charleston). Their large, light-filled shop on Worth Avenue features fine English antiques, silk pillows, French lanterns and pottery, Moroccan rugs and bags, and always a collection of beautiful books.

During "the season," Hammel and Edward Guffey entertain in a glorious and glamorous fashion at their Lake Worth home, a circa 1924 restored Mediterranean villa. They will often have a different group of guests in on consecutive evenings. The formal dining room is lit entirely by candles. Or perhaps they will host a small luncheon party outside, where they have two areas in which to entertain—poolside or the stunning Moorish-inspired garden.

Hammel skips from one shop to another with ease, checking on inventory, perfecting the displays, and chatting with customers (a very impressive list, I might add). While sitting in his Virginia office opening his mail on a quick, one-day stop in the dead of winter, he recounts the parties and the warm winter in Palm Beach. "It really is quite fun," he says simply.

Worth Avenue

This is particularly good on Bibb lettuce.

1/2 cup heavy cream
1 tablespoon lemon juice
1 cup mayonnaise
2 tablespoons tarragon vinegar
2 tablespoons garlic or shallot
    vinegar

2 tablespoons wine vinegar
1 tablespoon anchovy paste
2 tablespoons onion powder *or*
    1/4 cup chopped onion

Stir together lemon juice and cream. In another bowl combine other ingredients. Fold two mixtures together, just before serving salad. Makes $1\frac{3}{4}$ cups.

Palm Beach Lobster Salad Dressing

This is to be served by the butler in a large sterling silver bowl—poolside, of course.

---

2 tablespoons caviar
1 cup mayonnaise
1/2 cup catsup
1/2 cup chili sauce
1/2 cup chopped pimento
2 tablespoons chives

1 tablespoon parsley
1 tablespoon lemon juice
1 hard-boiled egg, chopped
Dash cayenne
Dash paprika
Salt and pepper to taste

Mix all ingredients and then chill. Makes 3 cups.

Mrs. Gotrock's Palm Beach Fruit Salad Dressing

This recipe is said to have come from one of Palm Beach's most famous hostesses, the late Marjorie Merriweather Post, who entertained lavishly at her winter home, Mar-A-Lago during the 1950s and 1960s. Designed by Marion Sims Wyeth and Joseph Urban in the 1920s, the home is now a private club owned by Donald Trump. Membership? $100,000.

2 ripe bananas
2 tablespoons lemon juice
1/4 cup brown sugar

1/4 cup honey
1 cup heavy cream, whipped

In food processor combine bananas, lemon juice, brown sugar, and honey until smooth. Then fold mixture into bowl of whipped cream. Serve over the following fruit salad:

1 cup watermelon balls
8 slices cantaloupe
8 slices Cranshaw melon
6–8 grapefruits, peeled and
  sectioned

16 orange sections
Bibb lettuce
Mint sprigs

Mound watermelon balls in center of silver platter lined with Bibb lettuce. Arrange remaining fruit around center like sun rays or any decorative arrangement. Garnish with mint sprigs. Serve dressing on side.

Lettuce Wedges à la Palm Beach

This one-step recipe is perfect for a large iceberg lettuce wedge as an accompaniment to a grilled sirloin steak, all served poolside, of course.

---

1 cup mayonnaise
1/4 cup Roquefort cheese
2 tablespoons cider vinegar
1/4 cup whipping cream

1 teaspoon Dijon mustard
1 clove garlic, crushed
1/4 teaspoon sage
Salt and pepper to taste

Blend together all ingredients with electric mixer on moderately low speed until smooth. Makes $1\frac{1}{2}$ cups.

Dressing for Roast Beef

This dressing also goes well when tossed with sliced cold prime rib of beef with pickled beets and served over a bed of Bibb lettuce.

1/4 cup snipped fresh dill
Snipped fresh chives
3 tablespoons drained horseradish
3 tablespoons lemon juice

3/4 cup sour cream
Ground salt to taste
Ground black pepper to taste

Whisk all together until smooth and consistent. Makes $1\frac{1}{4}$ cups.

Cucumber Dressing for Cold Poached Salmon

This is to be served with cold poached salmon on a bed of watercress.

---

1 cucumber, peeled, seeded, and
   chopped fine
1/2 cup sour cream
1/2 cup mayonnaise
1 tablespoon snipped fresh chives

1 teaspoon snipped fresh dill
1/2 teaspoon chopped parsley
Salt to taste
White pepper to taste
Fresh dill

Mix all ingredients and chill. Garnish with fresh dill. Makes $1\frac{1}{2}$ cups.

Ocala

From Palm Beach to Ocala is 239 miles into the middle of the State of Florida. Totally foreign to the seaside spots, it's horse country. Here, Nancy Stewart greets guests who are passing through for the horse show or looking for a show hunter from her husband, Don Stewart, a nationally known trainer and judge.

"As you can only imagine (knowing my husband), dinners, in the most cases, are unscheduled," she writes in a quick e-mail. "This, of course, is due to my husband's optimism that anything is possible! I try to have simple menus that can be whipped up quickly. Most people enjoy having 'home cooking' after being on the road so much; hence, that is my excuse for keeping it simple. A salad served with the main dish and a starch and a vegetable is more than enough for us tired horse show folks!"

Sesame Seed Dressing

Perfect on spinach with raw mushrooms and bamboo shoots. Add red peppers or red onions for a special touch.

1/4 teaspoon dry mustard	1 teaspoon Worcestershire sauce
1/2 teaspoon paprika	1 cup salad oil
1/2 teaspoon salt (optional)	1/2 cup cider vinegar
1/2 cup sugar	1/4 cup toasted sesame seeds

Mix together first five ingredients and beat well. Slowly add oil, and then gradually, a little bit at a time, add vinegar, beating constantly. Stir in sesame seeds. Makes 1 pint.

Special Dressing

2/3 cup oil
1/3 cup tarragon wine vinegar
1 clove garlic, minced
1 teaspoon salt

1/4 teaspoon dry basil
1/4 teaspoon dill
1/8 teaspoon white pepper
Dash Worcestershire sauce

Combine oil and vinegar in salad jar and then add remaining ingredients. Makes 1 cup.

FACTS ABOUT TOMATOES

According to the Web site www.floridatomatoes.org, while ripening, a tomato goes through six stages:

Green—The tomato surface is completely green. The shade of green may vary from light to dark.

Breakers—There is a definite break of color from green to tannish-yellow, pink or red on 10% or less of the tomato surface.

Turning—Tannish-yellow, pink or red color shows on over 10% but not more than 30% of the tomato surface.

Pink—Pink or red color shows on over 30% but not more than 60% of the tomato surface.

Light Red—Pinkish-red or red color shows on over 60% but red color covers not more than 90% of the tomato surface.

Red—Red color shows on over 90% of the tomato surface.

The site also offers these tips and facts:

Tomato Tips

Coring: Using a sharp paring knife make several angled cuts through the stem and under the core.

Seeding: Lay the tomato on its side and halve with a sharp serrated knife. Squeeze each half firmly enough to push out the seeds. Discard seeds.

Slicing: First core the tomato and lay it on its side. Using a sharp serrated knife, cut a very thin slice off both ends and discard. Slice the tomato to desired thickness.

Peeling: To eliminate the skin in cooked dishes, gently lower 2 or 3 tomatoes at a time into enough boiling water to cover. Boil for 15 to 30 seconds; lift into a colander with a slotted spoon. Rinse briefly under cold running water. Peel off and discard skins.

Stuffing Shells: Lay the tomato on its side and cut a very thin slice off the bottom using a sharp serrated knife. Slice off the top 1/4 of the tomato and discard. (The top minus the core [can] be chopped and added to the filling.) Using a sharp paring knife and spoon, cut and scoop out the flesh, leaving thickish walls. Salt the cavities lightly and invert on a cooling rack for 15 minutes to drain.

Yield: 1 medium tomato, seeded, yields approximately 3/4 cup chopped. 1 large tomato, seeded, yields 1 cup chopped. One pound of tomatoes yields approximately $2\frac{1}{2}$ cups of chopped or 2 cups puréed.

Storage: Tomatoes will ripen to a juicy red on their own when stored at room temperature. Refrigeration kills flavor in fresh tomatoes. _**Do not refrigerate tomatoes until fully ripe.**_

Florida Tomato Bits & Pieces

- Americans on average consume 17 pounds of tomatoes every year.

- Florida Tomatoes account for 95% of all U.S. grown tomatoes eaten by Americans October to June. And 45% of all tomatoes consumed in the U.S. year-round are Florida Tomatoes.

- Tomatoes are actually a fruit even though the U.S. Supreme Court declared them a vegetable in 1893. The tomato is a true American native. Originally cultivated by Aztecs and Incas as early as 700 A.D., tomatoes were introduced to Europeans during 16th century explorations.

Excerpted with permission from The Florida Tomato Committee (www.floridatomatoes.org).

Chapter 2

THE PEACH STATE

Georgia takes us into a new world of greens and ingredients. When Georgia is on my mind, I always think of Atlanta first.

Atlanta

Atlanta conjures up visions of the South in all its glory, . . . from the War between the States to *Gone with the Wind* and onward to the 1996 Olympic Games. Add to that mix the Civil Rights movement and a thriving cultural hub.

Stops along the way in this city should include the Atlanta History Center (with its thirty-three acres of gardens), Fernbank Museum of Natural History, The Margaret Mitchell House, and the splendid High Museum. Be sure to visit the Swan House, a circa 1928 mansion (with a collection of decorative arts from the late Philip Trammell Shutze, one of Atlanta's leading architects). The Tullie Smith Farm, circa 1845, is emblematic of Georgia's Piedmont area and named after a Civil War survivor. And, for children, don't miss the Victorian and Lee Playhouses. There are also plenty of salad tailgating opportunities in Atlanta, as sports thrive with the Braves, Falcons, Hawks, and Thrashers.

For retail therapy go to Lennox Square or Phipps Plaza.

For restaurants, the Buckhead Diner is one of the most popular and for good reason—upscale diner food such as the must-have "Southern Fried Chicken" with a hint of blackberries with sides of a Southern biscuit (what else?), beans, and mashed potatoes (with the traditional white gravy). Park your fat concerns outside, please. Or, perhaps you might try the salmon served with cheese grits, asparagus, and red onions. And I almost forgot...the diner's homemade potato chips with blue cheese are a specialty.

Fresh pasta is the taste at Veni Vidi Vici. A large suckling pig is usually on the rotisserie accompanied by warm and wonderful polenta and an array of breads with olive oil. The salads offered include the squid with lemon and salsa verde.

A little bit hokey but fun for the children, there's a restaurant called Pittypat's Porch, where a number of well-known politicians and sparklie types have visited since it opened in 1967. The name comes from the character of Aunt Pittypat Hamilton in *Gone with the Wind*. The décor can be described as antebellum, and I will not editorialize on that...really. But get this: the hostesses are dressed in *hoop skirts*! Never mind the food; there are drinks such as Pittypat's Pitch, a "brew of vodka, passion juice, and sacred herbs"; Scarlett's Passion, an adaptation of a frozen strawberry daiquiri; and (my favorite) The Ankle Breaker, described like this: "General Jackson broke his ankle after half a dozen of them. You might have to get yourself a partner to handle one." To which I say...okay. But, let's not forget the drink of choice in Atlanta...Coca-Cola. Most decent young girls have it for breakfast.

Piedmont Road
Dressing for Chopped Cucumbers

1 small onion, finely chopped
3/4 cup yogurt (or sour cream)
1 teaspoon prepared mustard
1 tablespoon vinegar

1/2 teaspoon salt
1/8 teaspoon pepper
1/2 teaspoon celery seed
Snipped fresh dill to taste

Mix together all ingredients and chill. Serve over cucumbers. Makes 1 cup.

Peachtree Road

This is good served over tossed green salad garnished with sprouts, toasted sesame seeds, mushrooms, and seedless raisins.

---

1 ripe avocado, peeled and mashed
1 cup yogurt
1 tablespoon soy sauce

1/8 teaspoon oregano
1/8 teaspoon pepper

Combine all ingredients and mix well. Makes $1\frac{1}{8}$ cups.

Simple Summer Salad at the Shore

My favorite salad would be with all kinds of greens, avocados, toasted almonds, and Mandarin oranges with some cold shrimp on the side.
—Jane Williamson

Jane Williamson is a Southern belle who owns an elegant interior decorating business in Atlanta. "Hang on, I'm coming to you," she says in a husky Southern enunciation while juggling call waiting one day.

She's been on the phone ordering "doorknobs, amber glass tiles to be set on the diagonal, and chocolate brown cabinets." Raised in North Carolina, Jane describes herself as "A Tar Heel at heart. It's in my blood." Her take on Southern salads includes vivid memories of the beach. "Barefoot in a bathing suit" is how she puts it. For many years she vacationed in South Litchfield, but more recently she spends a month at DeBordieu, both in South Carolina.

"Summer at the shore is informal. It's about sharing, it's not dealt out in little bowls," she explains. Rather, salad is served in an oversized bowl. (Knowing Jane it might even be something the size of a bucket, but it would be an elegant bucket you can count on that!) And it's to be served with a "big spoon and a spatula." She suggests that everyone get a Bloody Mary and then . . . "dig in and get it when you want."

1/2 cup olive oil
2 tablespoons minced onion
1 tablespoon Parmesan cheese
2 teaspoons salt
3/4 teaspoon Worcestershire sauce
3/4 teaspoon sugar

3/4 teaspoon dry mustard
3/4 teaspoon basil
3/4 teaspoon oregano
3/4 teaspoon pepper
1/4 cup red wine vinegar
1 tablespoon lemon juice

Put all ingredients into blender and mix. Makes 1 cup.

East Paces Ferry Road

Monday through Friday Lisa Newsom is busy as chairman and editor-in-chief of *Veranda* magazine in Atlanta. Her workdays are hectic and filled with meeting contacts and friends in the design industry. So when the weekend rolls around, she cherishes time spent with family whether it's at home, the seaside, or the mountains.

"One thing that's different here," she says one frenzied Monday morning, "is the growing season is so long. The gardens have a fall season, a winter season, early spring and summer, and it's all greens. We grow those heritage lettuces from Thomas Jefferson. And with so many varieties from Europe and Asia, the colors, shapes, and sizes make a presentation that sings. The visual impact is spectacular." (Just like her magazine.)

1/2 teaspoon salt	1/4 cup salad oil
Dash pepper	Dash red pepper sauce
2 tablespoons sugar	1 tablespoon snipped or dried
2 tablespoons vinegar	parsley

Mix together and pour over salad before serving. Serve with fresh greens, sliced cooked eggs, and beets. Makes 1/2 cup.

Chapter 3

THE PALMETTO STATE

Greenville

*L*ess than 150 miles north of Georgia is Greenville, South Carolina, pronounced by the locals as "Greenvull." It has been referred to as the rising star of the South. The visitors bureau tells us: "With the graceful Blue Ridge chain of the Appalachians only minutes from the heart of the city, the vitality that a growing number of international businesses brings into the city, and the elegance of stately, historic homes on tree-lined streets, Greenville offers a pleasing combination of gracious past and promising future.

Stops here should include the Greenville County Art Museum and the circa 1830 Beattie house. The two wings of the Italianate Gothic-style Beattie house were added as the family grew. And, although it has been relocated twice, it is now home to the Greenville Woman's Club. Be sure to see the Peace Center for the Performing Arts.

Not far from the arts center in the historic West End is the Reedy River Falls Historic Park, with two bubbling waterfalls and many walking and biking trails. It was here that the city had its start as an Indian trading station and mill, established about 1768, by Richard Pearis. In the late 1780s, Lemuel James Alston purchased a large chunk of land from a Colonel Thomas Brandon. In 1797, Alston designed the area, then called Pleasantburg. According to the experts of greater Greenville, "In 1815, he sold his

11,028 acres including the town then known as Greenville Court House, to Vardry McBeeunder, and eventually Greenville emerged as an antebellum trading center and summer resort."

By the mid-1800s, the Greenville & Columbia Railroad, Furman University, and the Greenville Female College had been built. And this was followed by a boom of cotton textile mills, which transformed this gracious town into a manufacturing hub. By 1917, it became known as the "Textile Center of the South."

Like many cities and towns (in the North and the South), there has been a rebirth in the downtown area, now lined with cafés, spacious walkways, and plazas with a European ambiance.

Pleasantburg Drive

Try with salad greens with grilled chicken, orange sections, and walnuts.

1/4 cup tarragon vinegar
1/4 cup oil
2 teaspoons sugar
2 tablespoons chutney, finely
 chopped

$1\frac{1}{2}$ teaspoons curry
 powder
Salt and pepper to taste

Combine all in jar and shake well. Makes 2/3 cup.

Dixie Russian Dressing

    Lib Shackelford has lived in Greenville for more than fifty years. She describes her salads as "old-fashioned." Very much like the family-owned grocery store called Eight O'clock, where she has shopped for years. Several friends even give bottles of salad dressing as Christmas gifts.

    "And any other thoughts on Southern salads?" I ask.

    She whispers one word: "Catsup."

    In the South there still exists an ever-so-elite group who insist on putting catsup on everything. This recipe should satisfy these folks. It should also be noted here that a pinch of salt is considered to be just a teeny-tiny bit!

---

1 14-ounce bottle of catsup
1 pint mayonnaise
2 small onions, chopped
3 teaspoons paprika
2 teaspoons curry powder

3 pinches salt
Juice of 3 lemons
5 drops Tabasco sauce
2 tablespoons honey

    Mix together all ingredients, stir well, and store in "icebox." Makes 4¼ cups—enough for an entire army. Need we say which one?

Caesar Salad Dressing

Lib Shackelford also prefers Caesar salad to all others. A traditional lady at heart, she uses the egg.

---

2 cloves garlic, minced
1 can (2 ounces) anchovy filets, drained
1/2 cup olive oil
1 tablespoon red wine vinegar
2 tablespoons lemon juice
1/2 teaspoon Worcestershire sauce

Pinch salt, optional
1/2 teaspoon dry mustard
1 egg, well beaten
Fresh grated Parmesan cheese
Fresh ground pepper
Rye croutons

In food processor mince garlic and anchovies, and then add next six ingredients. Pour mixture into bowl and whisk in beaten egg until thickened. Toss with romaine lettuce and then top with grated cheese, ground pepper, and rye croutons. Dressing is best when used immediately but can be stored in refrigerator. Makes 1 cup.

Caesar Salad Dressing without the Egg

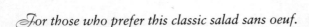

For those who prefer this classic salad sans oeuf.

1/4 cup lemon juice	1 tablespoon anchovy paste
1/4 cup water	1 teaspoon honey
1/4 cup cider vinegar	3 tablespoons grated Romano or
1/4 teaspoon salt	Parmesan cheese
1/4 teaspoon fresh ground pepper	3/4 cup oil
1 clove garlic, finely chopped	

Put everything (except oil) into blender. Blend until smooth on medium speed. Then while still blending, add oil in a slow, steady stream until mixture thickens. Chill. Makes $1\frac{1}{2}$ cups.

Augusta Road

One section of Greenville is known as the Augusta Road area. Be sure to visit the shops at The Plaza.

---

6 tablespoons blue cheese, crumbled
1/2 teaspoon Beau Monde seasonings
1/4 teaspoon salt

1/8 teaspoon garlic powder
1/4 teaspoon mustard
1/2 cup mayonnaise
1/2 cup cream
2 scallions, minced

Blend ingredients with fork and chill. Makes $1\frac{1}{2}$ cups.

Crescent Avenue

1 teaspoon paprika	1 teaspoon grated onion
1 teaspoon celery seed	1/2 cup vegetable oil
1 teaspoon dry mustard	1/2 cup vinegar
1 teaspoon salt	

Combine all ingredients in glass jar and cover tightly. Shake to mix and then chill for several hours before serving over salad. Makes $1\frac{3}{4}$ cups.

Crescent Salad

Try this one when the ladies come over for lunch or at the garden club meeting.

2 small heads Bibb lettuce, washed and torn
1 pound fresh spinach, washed and torn
2 oranges, peeled, seeded, and sectioned

1/2 medium onion (red preferred), sliced into rings
1/2 cup coarsely chopped walnuts
2 tablespoons butter

Sauté walnuts in butter and then toss together with lettuce, spinach, oranges, and onion and add dressing. Makes 8 servings.

Honey Poppy Seed Dressing

This is an excellent low-fat dressing. It goes well with (that Southern favorite) fruit and is also good on smoked turkey.

3/4 cup plain nonfat yogurt
3 tablespoons honey

2 teaspoons lemon juice
1 teaspoon poppy seeds

Combine all ingredients in jar and chill. Makes 1 cup.

Charleston

From Greenville we travel 212 miles to Charleston, smack dab on the Atlantic Coast (and the site of Hurricane Hugo's appearance and destruction in 1989). It's known as the low country of South Carolina with a poised and polished way of life... slow and enchanting. A mixture of English, Irish, French, Spanish, German, Swiss, Santo Domingan, African, Native American, and Caribbean influences is found throughout. The most noteworthy power is the British, who became the first English settlers in the spring of 1670. "Charles Towne" was first named in honor of King Charles II.

As the English port and its merchant-planter aristocracy grew, the town developed into a small city. Today it is portrayed as "a place where the past is still present... where gas lit lamps flicker in warm southern breezes and cobblestone streets pave the way to intriguing boutiques and exquisite dining."

While visiting you will come across story-telling attractions, pristine beaches, and world-class golf. (Get your retail fix along King Street.) There are carriage tours, walking tours, nature tours, and garden tours. The celebrated cuisine consists of fresh seafood and favorites such as shrimp and grits or Frogmore Stew (see also www.charlestoncvb.com).

Spicy Shrimp over Fried Green Tomatoes

One of the most sought-out reservations in Charleston is at Circa 1886. Set in a carriage house at the Wentworth Mansion, it is under the eye of Chef Marc Collins. The dishes are inspired by Southern traditions with a contemporary twist. A graduate of the Pennsylvania Institute of Culinary Arts in Pittsburgh, Chef Collins was formerly the executive chef at the Fairmont Hotel in San Antonio, Texas (more info at www.circa1886.com). He offers us this delectable salad dish. And for dessert, how about Carolina Gold Rice Pudding or Pan-Fried Angel Food Cake?

Marinade

9 shrimp	3/4 cup canola oil
1 small shallot, peeled	1 teaspoon salt
2 cloves garlic, peeled	1 pinch white pepper
1/8 cup red hot sauce	

Place shallots, garlic, and red hot sauce in blender and blend until smooth. Slowly add oil to mixture while it is still blending. Season to taste and refrigerate. Let shrimp marinate in this mixture for about a half hour.

Fried Green Tomatoes

1/2 cup corn flour
1/2 cup all-purpose flour
2 tablespoons Old Bay Seasoning

1 cup buttermilk
1 green tomato

Heat fryer oil to 350 degrees. Slice green tomato about 1/2-inch thick. Mix both flours and Old Bay Seasoning together. Place tomato in flour mixture to completely coat it. Next place it in buttermilk and then back into flour mixture. Place into fryer and cook until golden brown. Take out shrimp and grill until done (about 3 minutes per side). Arrange shrimp on top of fried green tomato and place this over fresh tomato sauce. Serve immediately. Serves 3.

East Bay

1 tablespoon fresh tarragon	1 cup oil
1 tablespoon fresh parsley	1/4 cup cider vinegar
1 tablespoon fresh chives	1/2 teaspoon dry mustard
1 tablespoon fresh chervil	Sea salt and fresh ground pepper to
1 tablespoon fresh dill	taste

Shake all ingredients together in cruet and chill. Makes $1\frac{1}{2}$ cups. Serve with Nicoise Salad or mixed cooked and chilled vegetables.

Nicoise Salad

Fresh tomatoes, cut into quarters	String beans, blanched, chilled, and cut
New potatoes, cooked, chilled, and diced	Red leaf lettuce
	Tuna fish, drained

Combine tomatoes, new potatoes, and string beans in bowl. Toss with red leaf lettuce, tuna fish, and dressing above.

Thyme for Tomatoes

In the South pronounced TOE-MAAA-TOES.

---

2 teaspoons fresh thyme (or 1
   teaspoon dry)
1/4 cup white wine vinegar
1 tablespoon plus 1 teaspoon Dijon
   mustard

3 cloves garlic, minced
2 teaspoons salt
Lots of fresh ground pepper
1/4 cup peanut oil
3/4 cup olive oil

Put first six ingredients in food processor or blender and then add oil in a slow and steady stream. Serve over fresh-from-the-garden tomatoes. Makes $1\frac{1}{2}$ cups.

Sweet Southern Dressing

1/4 cup sugar
1/2 cup finely chopped onions
1/4 cup cider vinegar
1/2 teaspoon salt

1/2 teaspoon dry mustard
1/4 teaspoon celery seed
1/8 teaspoon pepper
1/2 cup oil

Combine first seven ingredients in food processor or blender and mix well. With machine running, gradually pour in oil. Chill well. Perks up iceberg lettuce perfectly! Or try:

Meeting Street Salad

Romaine lettuce
Tomato quarters

Julienne of sweet red peppers

Mustard Vinaigrette

Éleanor Taylor grew up in Raleigh and now lives in Charleston with her husband, Van. She has made a salad for dinner every night of their thirty years of married life. "This always comes into play," Eleanor says. "We are now on a diet all the time so I use a lot of greens, spring onions, and tomatoes."

"He thinks it's not dinner without a salad," Eleanor says. So her creativity has run wild through the years. Her philosophy is, "If I'm going to serve it, it's going to be pretty. We're into presentation down here. If you're having dinner you're having salad. I have nine bags of salad greens in the refrigerator right now." Her standby dressing is the Mustard Vinaigrette.

---

2 tablespoons Dijon mustard	1/4 teaspoon salad herbs
3/4 cup olive oil	1/8 teaspoon tarragon
3 teaspoons fresh lemon juice	1/4 teaspoon salt
5 teaspoons white vinegar	Pinch sugar
1/4 teaspoon pressed garlic	

Mix all ingredients in glass cruet and shake well. Chill. Makes 1 cup.

Chapter 4

THE TAR HEEL STATE

Raleigh

From Charleston to Raleigh (pronounced Raw-lee) is 285 miles north. Often referred to as a park within a city, Raleigh has been identified for its "Trees, Tees, and PhDs." There are more than one hundred gardens, parks, and open spaces. Oak trees reign supreme, and at Moore Square Park, a visitor will spot a copper acorn. At Pullen Park, there's a stunning 1911 Gustave A. Dentzel Menagerie Carousel as well as paddleboats and a train.

During the 1700s, politicians met in a number of different cities to do their business, and Raleigh was just one of them. Then, in the late 1780s it was decided that the state capital must be recognized within ten miles of Isaac Hunter's plantation in Wake County. The city was officially acknowledged in 1792 and named for Sir Walter Raleigh, illustrious for founding the first English colony in the New World (on the Outer Banks of North Carolina).

Raleigh is one of the three U.S. capitals designed on paper prior to being developed. Places to see include the 1840 Greek Revival style State Capitol building, the North Carolina Museum of Art, the North Carolina Museum of History, and the circa 1891 30-room North Carolina Executive Mansion. Also, check out the State Farmer's Market, where annual events include the North Carolina Battle of the Sauces and a Chili Fest. (I told you Southerners are serious in the kitchen.)

Put Tyler House at the Lassiter at North Hills on top of your list...this ladies specialty shop features accessories, sportswear, and gifts. (You will also meet my fabulous friend Tot Williams there.) There's more good shopping at Cameron Village, where a local "expert" advises shoppers to visit Lavender and Lace, Charlotte's, and Bailey's Jewelers. A must-see antique shop is Edith Medlin's shop in Glenwood Village, where you can also grab a bite at the Glenwood Grill.

And finally, you haven't seen a tailgate party in a parking lot until you've been to Raleigh...there are four professional sports teams and seven key colleges and universities. Basketball is a religion in these parts. Envision a sea of N.C. State Wolfpack fans all dressed in red: "Go Staaaaaaaayt."

Hales Road Dressing

There are some people who just ooze style—JoAnn Shea is one of them. For many years she was the on-site floral designer for Devonshire in Middleburg, Virginia. Her massive springtime arrangements of lilacs would bring tears to my eyes. Now living in Raleigh, she and husband Jim often have salad for lunch.

"I know you may have heard of this," she says, "but how about Romaine lettuce, pears, Feta cheese, and pecans?" The pecans add the Southern touch. Or, she adds, "Try dried cranberries." All of the ingredients come fresh from the local grocery store, Harris Teeter, referred to by the locals as "HT."

1/2 cup raspberry vinegar
1 tablespoon lemon juice
1½ teaspoons pepper
1 teaspoon salt
1/2 teaspoon sugar

1/2 teaspoon dry mustard
1½ teaspoons Worcestershire sauce
1 clove garlic, minced
1½ cups salad oil

Combine all ingredients in glass salad jar and chill. Makes 2¼ cups.

Tomato Aspic

Gwen Spann grew up in Smithfield, Virginia, and now lives in Charlotte, where she runs a showroom called G. George Designer. As a busy woman, she says, "I find salads for parties difficult, as a good tossed salad or Caesar is a bitch in terms of time and to keep from wilting. Tossed salads take up too much room on a plate, so they necessitate a separate salad plate and I don't know where you live, but help isn't as plentiful as it used to be. I personally prefer good old Southern Tomato Aspic. It is unexpected, can be made ahead, doesn't take up much room on a buffet plate." (Note: What sets this one apart is the distinctive Caper and Caviar Dressing.)

---

1 package (6 ounce) lemon Jello
1/2 cup boiling water
1 can (29 ounce) tomato sauce

1/4 cup cider vinegar
Several dashes Worcestershire sauce
Several dashes Tabasco sauce

Dissolve Jello in boiling water and add remaining ingredients. Pour into ring mold and let jell. Remove from mold and top with Caper and Caviar Dressing. Serves 8–10.

Caper and Caviar Dressing for Tomato Aspic

2 cups mayonnaise
1/2 cup small capers, drained
Dash ground red pepper

1 teaspoon lemon juice
2 ounces black caviar

Place mayonnaise in small bowl (to fit inside aspic ring) and stir in capers, red pepper, and lemon juice. Place bowl in center of aspic ring on serving plate and mound heaping spoonfuls of caviar on top of caper mayonnaise. Makes $2\frac{1}{2}$ cups.

Shrimp and Cantaloupe Salad

Cot Williams wins the prize in the Southern accent contest. I hope someone invites me to be on television with this book so I can bring her along. Nobody would believe how she "tawks." She tells me salads have gotten more "sophisticated":

"Down here we're loving salads with strawberries and chicken and walnuts. I like to make a salad that's ready and I can pop it out." She speaks of blueberries, strawberries, and "great big hunks of chicken" with romaine lettuce, raspberry dressing, and "gandazula (Gorgonzola) or whatever you call it."

The bottom line? Adding fruit to an otherwise ordinary salad will definitely move it up a notch or two. Try this one:

Dressing

1/2 cup vegetable oil	2 tablespoons lemon juice
2 tablespoons vinegar	1/4 teaspoon curry powder
2 tablespoons chopped chutney	Pinch pepper
1/4 teaspoon salt	

Combine all ingredients in small bowl and mix well. Makes 7/8 cup.

Salad

3/4 pound shrimp, cooked and peeled
1/2 medium avocado, peeled, cubed, and sprinkled with lemon juice

1/2 cup slivered water chestnuts
1 large cantaloupe, peeled and cubed
Romaine lettuce leaves

Toss shrimp with avocado and water chestnuts. To serve, arrange cantaloupe on romaine lettuce, spoon shrimp mixture over cantaloupe, and then spoon dressing over all. Serves 4.

FACTS ABOUT CUCUMBERS

Few would ever associate the cucumber with the Tar Heel State, but cucumbers are grown all across North Carolina. Most of them are grown near the coast, but they are grown in the mountains too. The well-drained soil of the coastal region is perfect for growing cucumbers.

The North Carolina Vegetable Growers Association represents many different types of vegetables. One of these is the cucumber. There are two basic types of cucumbers grown in North Carolina. These are slicing or fresh market cucumbers and pickling cucumbers. Examples of slicing cucumber varieties include Centurian, Dasher II, Guardian, General Lee, Marketmore 76, Poinsett 76, and Revenue.

Believed to be from India originally, the cucumber was brought to North Carolina sometime in the mid-1500s. The Spaniards, who then taught Native Americans how to grow European vegetables, probably brought cucumbers to North America.

Technological advances such as harvesting machines have affected the cucumber industry, but in North Carolina nearly all of the crop is still harvested by hand. Because it has become so popular, there are new varieties that are able to resist diseases. When buying cucumbers select firm, well-shaped ones. Do not pick those that are yellowish, soft, or withered looking.

In North Carolina, officials select cucumbers at random and grade them using USDA guidelines. This is then applied to the crop. The samples are inspected for size, grade, defects, shape, and color. The grades for cucumbers are U.S. Fancy, U.S. Extra 1, U.S. 1, U.S. 1 Small, U.S. 1 Large, and U.S. 2.

Chapter 5

THE OLD DOMINION

$\mathscr{S}$tately Virginia is my home state now. I live in the horse country around Middleburg, Virginia, but love to explore the whole state.

Richmond

Virginia's state capital was named after the London suburb of Richmond. It was first the site of the Powhatan Indian Confederacy, but by 1607, the British, led by Christopher Newport, appeared. The area expanded as a trading post for fur and tobacco. It was officially founded in 1737 by Colonel William Byrd II, became a town in 1742 (population of 250), and was named as the capital in 1782.

Grand is a word that comes to mind for this glorious city with wide, sweeping boulevards and avenues. Take a drive up Monument Avenue to gaze at the splendid statues of such Confederates as Matthew Fontaine Maury, General Thomas J. (Stonewall) Jackson, Jefferson Davis, General Robert E. Lee, and General J.E.B. Stuart, joined in 1996 by Richmond's favorite son tennis legend Arthur Ashe.

Places to visit? Check out neighborhoods like Shockoe Slip, Oregon Hill, and The Fan. Stop by the Valentine Museum, Lewis Ginter Botanical Garden, the Virginia Museum of Fine Arts (a lovely collection of Fabergé eggs here along with a large collection of equine art from the late Paul Mellon), Edgar Allan Poe Museum, Hollywood Cemetery, and the White House of the

Confederacy. And then there's St. John's Church, where Patrick Henry made his famous speech in 1775.

But don't let the cobblestone streets, big old houses, and gas lamps fool you. This is a very sophisticated city, especially when it comes to food. The restaurants and chefs here are serious.

Erroll Somay, head of the Virginia Newspaper Project at the Virginia State Library, grew up in Virginia and North Carolina. After graduating from UNC, he lived for a while in New York before settling down in Richmond. Anyone knows that the food up North in the big city is supposed to be the best. Erroll ticks off the names of restaurants in Richmond: Edo's Squid, Mamma Zu, and Sweetwater's (not the chain). At a Chinese restaurant called Full Kee, he says the fresh fish is so good that "it knocks me out."

There is a definite geographical divergence with salads and cooking Erroll says. "In New York, when you turn on the stove, the cockroaches run out." As a child he remembers ambrosia, yet another Southern staple: fruit (either canned or fresh) with coconut, mini marshmallows, and sour cream.

"The fact that there are salads is a distinction," Erroll says. "In New York City on the buffet line or in the Old World eating establishments of my youth in the Midwest at the smorgasbords, it was meat and potatoes."

Le Rat's Spinach Salad Dressing

This comes from a restaurant that was once in Middleburg. It's to be served over a salad of spinach, bacon bits, sliced purple onion, and pecan halves.

---

1 or 2 teaspoons bacon drippings
3 tablespoons oil
1 tablespoon wine vinegar
2 tablespoons brown sugar

2 tablespoons Dijon mustard
2 shakes Worcestershire sauce
Lots of fresh ground pepper

Heat bacon drippings in small skillet and then stir in remaining ingredients. Heat just enough to melt sugar and blend flavors. Makes 2/3 cup.

Virginia All-Season Salad Dressing

Toss with iceberg lettuce, chopped celery, beets, and chopped Virginia ham. Serve with chilled white wine and baking soda biscuits.

---

1 cup vegetable oil
1/3 cup red wine vinegar
2 tablespoons Dijon mustard
1 teaspoon salt
2 tablespoons sugar

$1\frac{1}{2}$ teaspoons pepper
3/4 teaspoon dried tarragon
1 teaspoon Tabasco sauce
Parsley flakes

Whisk together oil and vinegar. Add remaining ingredients and chill. Makes $1\frac{1}{2}$ cups.

Middleburg

Barbara and William Scott live at Svea Farm near Middleburg, Virigina. They are apple aficionados. The Scotts began their journey into the world of fruit in the late 1980s by planting all kinds of apple trees.

"You name it," William says. "If they didn't fruit well, I uprooted them and went on." Among their first attempts was Cox's Orange Pippin. "This is one of the most famous of English apple trees," Barbara explains, "but it just wouldn't do here." But they did discover that the Gala, a scion of Cox's Orange Pippin, would flourish.

The Scotts have learned to appreciate that most American apple trees came from seedlings as opposed to the more aristocratic European hybridized species. They have also determined that the apple trees originating from Northern Italy, Southern France, Southern Germany, and the Middle East do best in Middleburg. They now have two hundred varieties of heirloom apples, pears, peaches, plums, cherries, apricots, grapes, gooseberries, raspberries, and strawberries.

William keeps copious handwritten notes on the subject of fruit trees. And he tells anyone who is interested that trees dripping with fruit don't just happen. "You must address the nutrients needed. Take your leaves to the local extension agent each August. Give the trees what they lack, don't just add nitrogen."

"And have the trees pruned correctly," he adds. "Read up on the subject and talk to the experts."

A few trees among the Scott's collection include Early Joe (c. 1800 New York); Holstein (c. 1935 Germany); Kandil Sinap (c. 1801 Turkey); the wonderful Lady apple developed by Louis XIII (c. 1628 France); Orleans Reinettes (c. 1776 France); Golden Nugget (c. 1932 Nova Scotia); and one of Thomas Jefferson's favorites, the Albemarle Pippin (c. 1750 New York).

The Scotts adore sharing and evaluating their abundance with friends. Several times a year, at different harvest dates, they entertain.

In the fall, they have an apple-crushing party. Crates of apples wait for guests alongside an antique hand-turned cider press. The Scotts use a "recipe" they found in an old journal: 50 percent Golden Delicious "for the most complex group of flavors," with 25 percent Empire "because it makes a lot of juice and is very tart," and 25 percent Nittany for the "combination of sweet and acid."

The guests enjoy sips of fresh cider in the afternoon. But the real fun begins at dinner, when previous years' cider is served as crisp and glistening wine. (The secret cider recipe also contains a touch of crabapple for "the astringent and drying qualities.") More handwritten notes (done with a real ink pen—rare these days) are kept in the basement/wine cellar.

Barbara puts together a complementary menu (color is important to all Southern cooks too) of roasted pork; acorn squash; and a salad of red leaf lettuce, apples (of course), walnuts, and dressed perfectly with a ginger dressing.

Ginger Salad Dressing

This is magnificent with salad greens tossed with apples (Barbara Scott suggests Gala apples) or pear slices.

2-inch piece ginger, peeled and
  grated
3 cloves garlic, minced
2 tablespoons Dijon mustard
2 tablespoons honey

$1\frac{1}{2}$ teaspoons salt
1/2 teaspoon fresh ground pepper
1/4 cup cider vinegar
3/4 cup salad oil

Combine all ingredients and mix well. Makes $1\frac{3}{4}$ cups.

Chapter 6

DOWN IN THE GARDEN

In the South, we have always used vegetables like potatoes, cabbage, etc. in our salads as staples. We also use fruits like apples, oranges frequently for "color" as well as flavor.

—Gwen Spann, Charlotte, North Carolina

Dilled Summer Squash Salad

3/4 pound zucchini, cut into
   paper-thin slices
3/4 pound yellow summer squash,
   cut into paper-thin slices
$1\frac{1}{2}$ teaspoons salt

1/3 cup white vinegar
3/4 cup sugar
1 tablespoon snipped fresh dill
Fresh ground pepper

In colander toss zucchini and yellow squash with salt and let drain at least 1 hour. Then refresh squash under cold running water and drain well. In large glass bowl combine vinegar and sugar, stirring until sugar is dissolved. Add squash, dill, and pepper and combine well. Chill salad covered at least 2 hours or overnight. Serves 6.

Dressing for Cauliflower-Broccoli Salad

2/3 cup mayonnaise
1/3 cup buttermilk
2 teaspoons celery seed
1 cup chopped green or purple
  onion

Salt and pepper to taste
Dash Tabasco sauce

Combine all ingredients. Toss with $2\frac{1}{2}$ cups of chopped fresh broccoli and $2\frac{1}{2}$ cups chopped fresh cauliflower. Chill. Makes 1 cup and serves 6.

Fresh Dandelion Salad

If you are skeptical about dandelion's strong flavor, start only with the very youngest early spring leaves, before the flowers have formed. When cutting wild dandelions from your lawn or fields, make certain they have not been sprayed with weed killer or fertilizer! Dandelion greens are good uncooked tossed with French dressing, chopped green onions, chopped hard-boiled eggs, crumbled crisp bacon, anchovies, and pimentos.

3/4 to 1 pound young, fresh
   dandelion greens
2 tablespoons olive oil
2 tablespoons lemon juice
1 clove garlic, pressed

Salt and pepper to taste
2 ounces Feta cheese, crumbled
1 tomato, cut into wedges
Few ripe olives

Wash dandelion greens thoroughly and trim ends. Cook in 2 quarts of boiling water until stems are tender crisp, about 5 minutes. Drain and rinse in cold water, and drain again. Place on paper towel to absorb excess water. Arrange on platter and set aside.

Combine olive oil, lemon juice, garlic, salt, and pepper. Drizzle over greens. Cover and refrigerate until serving time. Sprinkle with Feta cheese and garnish with tomato wedges and olives. Serves 4.

Orange Avocado Salad

1 tablespoon salad oil
2 tablespoons chopped fresh
  cilantro
1 tablespoon chopped green onion

2 tablespoons fresh lime juice
1/4 teaspoon salt
1/4 teaspoon sugar
1/8 teaspoon fresh ground pepper

Combine all ingredients in blender and blend well. Chill. Makes 1/2 cup.

Peel and slice two ripe avocados and two oranges. Arrange on a bed of Bibb lettuce. Serves 4.

Peanut Butter–Sesame Dressing

What could be more Southern than a peanut butter dressing? Serve over fresh pasta, and to complete the dinner (which is great for late summer suppers on the deck) serve with cold, cooked (fresh from the garden) broccoli and carrots. Add some mini blueberry muffins (my favorite). The entire meal can be made in advance. Serves 2 as the main course or 4 as a side dish.

1/2 cup peanut butter
1/2 cup water
3 tablespoons soy sauce
1 tablespoon rice wine vinegar

2 teaspoons sesame oil
1 teaspoon grated fresh ginger
1 medium garlic clove, minced
1/4 teaspoon ground red pepper

Combine all ingredients in blender and blend until smooth. Chill. Makes $1\frac{1}{4}$ cups.

Cook and drain 6 ounces of linguine, blanche 4 ounces of snow peas, and chop 3 scallions. You may also add sliced water chestnuts. Toss with dressing.

Tangy Cream Dressing for Pea Salad

1/4 teaspoon garlic powder
1/2 teaspoon salt
$1\frac{1}{2}$ teaspoons sugar
3 tablespoons red wine vinegar

4 teaspoons milk
1/2 cup sour cream
Dash dry mint flakes (optional)

Mix all ingredients and chill overnight. Makes 7/8 cup.

Pea Salad

According to two of my food consultants and friends, Jennifer Aldrich and Louise Sinclaire, fresh peas, if they are really fresh, are always best, but make sure they are used promptly and not overcooked. However, fresh peas are a Southern rarity, because they disappear or turn very starchy as soon as the days and nights heat up. This is why one often hears talk of frozen peas. Frozen peas really do not need to be cooked if they are small.

---

10 ounces fresh peas, blanched *or* 10 ounces frozen peas, thawed and patted dry	Sliced water chestnuts, drained 1/4 cup scallions 6 slices cooked bacon, crumbled

---

Toss together all salad ingredients and then add Tangy Cream Dressing to taste. Chill before serving. Serves 4.

Just for Brussel Sprout Lovers

There are very few of us!

1/4 teaspoon dry dill
1/2 teaspoon Dijon mustard
1 small clove garlic, minced
1 tablespoon chopped fresh parsley

2 tablespoons finely chopped onion
2 tablespoons red wine vinegar
6 tablespoons olive oil

Combine ingredients in small bowl with large slotted spoon. Toss with 8 ounces of brussel sprouts that have been cooked and sliced in half. Put sprouts and dressing in large sealed jar and chill overnight. Serve on romaine lettuce leaves. Makes 1 cup and serves 4.

Parsley Dressing for Chickpea Salad

1 clove garlic
1 ounce anchovy fillets, drained
  well
1 hard-boiled egg, peeled and
  quartered
1/8 cup sherry wine vinegar
1 tablespoon Dijon mustard

1 tablespoon lemon juice
1/2 teaspoon dry thyme
1/2 teaspoon ground bay leaves
1/2 cup minced fresh parsley
3 tablespoons olive oil
Fresh ground black pepper

With food processor or blender running add garlic, anchovies, and egg. Then add vinegar, mustard, lemon juice, thyme, and bay leaves and puree. Blend in parsley and oil and add pepper to taste. Makes $1\frac{1}{2}$ caps.

Chickpea Salad

15 ounces garbanzo beans, drained
  well

1/4 cup chopped onion

Toss together beans and onions with dressing. Chill before serving. Serves 4.

FACTS ABOUT CARROTS

According to the fabulous, fun Web site www.carrotmuseum.com:

The bright orange fleshy root vegetable we know today as the carrot is a far cry from its wild ancestor, a small tough, pale fleshed acrid root plant. The Wild Carrot—Daucus Carota—is one of the many plants which belongs to the natural order Umbelliferae. It is a common plant in pastures and by roadsides and especially likes light soils where it can soon turn into a weed. It has a long history.

To unravel the history of the Carrot you have to go back a very long way. It originated some 5000 years ago in Middle Asia around Afghanistan, and slowly spread into the Mediterranean area. The first carrots were white, purple, red, yellow, green and black—not orange. Its roots were thin and turnip coloured. Temple drawings from Egypt in 2000 B.C. show a plant some Egyptologists believe to represent a large carrot. Egyptian papyruses contain information about treatment with carrot and its seeds were found in pharaoh crypts. Carrot seeds have been found in prehistoric Swiss lake dwellings giving clear evidence of human consumption. There is however no evidence of cultivation at this stage, more likely they were used for medicinal purposes. Similar findings appear also in ancient Glastonbury. Neolithic people savoured the roots of the wild carrot for its sweet, succulent flavour.

Another Web site, www.aboutproduce.com, recommends avoiding "flabby, soft, or wilted carrots or product that shows any mildew, decay, growth cracks, or splits." It states, "Good quality carrots should be well-shaped with firm, smooth exteriors. Color should be vibrant orange to orange-red. For best quality, tops should be closely trimmed since they tend to decay rapidly."

And there is the very important beta carotene content: mature carrots have over 50 percent more of this anticancer benefit than their smaller version.

Finally, a bit of carrot trivia: In Europe, the feather-like stems were once used to adorn hats and other fashionable hairstyles. It is the second most popular vegetable in the world, after the potato.

Chapter 7

NINE VERSIONS OF SOUTHERN PASSION: MAYO

INCLUDING ONE FOR THOSE WHO WANT TO CHEAT!

Bayou

---

2 tablespoons dry mustard	1 cup milk
2 tablespoons flour	1/4 cup vinegar
3/4 cup sugar	2 egg yolks, beaten
1 teaspoon salt	

Combine dry ingredients in saucepan, add milk and vinegar, and cook over low heat until thick. Add beaten egg yolks and continue to cook over medium heat until very thick. Chill overnight. Makes $1\frac{1}{2}$ cups.

Upland

Try with Algonquin Salad, a mix of romaine lettuce, grapefruit, fresh pears, and green peppers.

1/2 cup buttermilk
1 cup mayonnaise
1/2 cup catsup
1/2 teaspoon Worcestershire sauce
1 teaspoon paprika

Dash garlic powder
Salt to taste
1/2 teaspoon parsley flakes
Fresh ground pepper

Stir buttermilk and mayonnaise together and mix well. Add remaining ingredients and chill. Makes 1 pint.

Meadow Mayo

Try with Paulette Salad, a mix of cold cooked asparagus tips, string beans, and artichokes with endive.

---

1 large tablespoon fresh cracked
  pepper
1/8 teaspoon Tabasco sauce
1/4 teaspoon steak sauce
1 cup mayonnaise
2 tablespoons water
1/2 teaspoon lemon juice

1/2 teaspoon Worcestershire sauce
1/4 teaspoon dry mustard
1/4 teaspoon sugar
1/2 teaspoon salt
1/4 teaspoon garlic powder
Grated Parmesan to taste

In small bowl, combine pepper, Tabasco sauce, and steak sauce. Blend with mayonnaise and add remaining ingredients. Chill well before serving, at least 3 hours. Makes $1\frac{1}{4}$ cups.

Piedmont

2 tablespoons wine vinegar
1 teaspoon dry mustard
1/2 cup Dijon mustard
3 shallots, finely chopped
3 tablespoons peanut oil
3/4 cup mayonnaise

1 tablespoon curry powder, or to
  taste
2 tablespoons lime juice
3 tablespoons sour cream
1 tablespoon chives, chopped

Combine vinegar, mustards, and shallots in bowl. Gradually add peanut oil, mixing well with wire whisk. Add mayonnaise and curry powder, mixing well. Whisk in lime juice, then sour cream and chives. Refrigerate overnight. Makes 1 pint.

Mountain Mayo

This translates to Southern as Green Mayo for Beef.

---

20 ounces fresh spinach	2 tablespoons fresh dill
1 bunch watercress	2 tablespoons fresh chives
2 cups mayonnaise	2 tablespoons fresh tarragon
Juice of 1 lemon	2 tablespoons fresh chervil

Wash and remove stems of spinach and watercress and rough chop. Put into blender or food processor with some of the mayonnaise and reduce to a puree. Place mixture in bowl with rest of mayonnaise and mix well. Stir in lemon juice (2 tablespoons of dry white wine can be substituted for lemon juice, if preferred) and herbs and chill. Makes 8–10 servings.

Mangrove Mayo

1 cup mayonnaise	3/4 teaspoon granulated garlic
1 cup buttermilk	3/4 teaspoon celery salt
1 tablespoon marjoram	3/4 teaspoon granulated onion
1 tablespoon basil	$1\frac{1}{2}$ teaspoons brown sugar

Mix together and beat well to blend. Chill well in glass jar. Stores well in refrigerator. Makes $2\frac{1}{4}$ cups.

Fall Line
(Cheater's "Homemade" Mayonnaise)

This will fool any significant other!

---

1 jar (16 ounce) Hellman's
  mayonnaise
1 mayonnaise capful of cider
  vinegar
1 teaspoon dry mustard

Dash seasoned salt or celery salt
Lots of seasoned pepper
Dash garlic powder
$1\frac{1}{2}$ teaspoons celery seed
2 teaspoons paprika

Blend well and put into another jar that does not resemble a Hellman's jar. Cover and chill.

Tidewater Mayo

This one came from my friend Claudia Young in Virginia. She is an artist in the kitchen. It's best made with Hellman's. This recipe is similar to an old-fashioned Boiled Bacon Dressing. It's wonderful on garden lettuce or spinach. This makes quite a lot—enough to feed all the farm hands—so feed a crowd or share with a friend, although it will keep covered in the "icebox."

1 pound bacon
1 medium onion, grated
1 cup sugar (or less for a dressing
  not so sweet)
1/2 cup cider vinegar

1 tablespoon bacon drippings
  (optional)
1/2 cup water
Fresh ground pepper
1 quart mayonnaise

Fry bacon until crisp; drain and set aside. Then brown onion in bacon drippings and drain and set aside. Pour off excess grease and add to skillet (cast iron preferred in this case!) sugar, vinegar, bacon drippings, water, and pepper. Bring to boil; stir to dissolve sugar and then cool. When cool, mix with 1 quart of mayonnaise, crumbled bacon, and onion.

Everglades Mayo

This is good with fruit cocktail (that's right, the good old-fashioned kind right from the can) and cottage cheese in the winter. Or in the summer with pineapple slices with grated sharp cheese on lettuce. It also goes well with The Silver Palm, a mix of hearts of romaine, sliced bananas, raisins, and sweet peppers.

---

1 jar of your favorite store-bought
   mayonnaise
Dash nutmeg

Dash ginger
Juice of canned fruit

Mix together mayonnaise, nutmeg, and ginger. Add enough fruit juice to get desired consistency. Shake well.

Chapter 8

THE CLASSICS

*H*ow never to get caught undressed . . . standbys to turn to every day. In the South, when a woman tells her friend she's having an affair, it means she's hosting a charity event. However, as one friend begged to divulge, "When it comes down to it, all affairs end up being charity."

French Number One

This one is rather sweet. Good on lettuce or fruit.

Juice of 1 lemon
1/2 cup vegetable oil
1 cup sugar
2/3 cup catsup
1/3 teaspoon salt

1/2 cup white vinegar
1/2 onion, grated
Fresh ground pepper
1/2 teaspoon celery seed

Put all ingredients in electric blender and mix for 5 minutes. Makes 1 pint.

Simple French Dressing

This is a good basic dressing, an insurance against being caught undressed—that is, having to use bottled dressing in front of company!

---

1 cup olive oil	1/2 teaspoon pepper
2 tablespoons wine vinegar	1/4 teaspoon dry mustard
1 teaspoon salt	1 teaspoon garlic powder

Combine all ingredients in jar and cover and shake well. Keeps well in refrigerator. Makes $1\frac{1}{4}$ cups.

To this basic dressing you can add a bit of blue cheese or herbs. Lemon juice can be substituted for wine vinegar.

Other ideas and variations:

Capers: Add 2 teaspoons chopped.
Celery seed: Add 1/2 teaspoon.
Chili powder: Omit dry mustard and add 1/4 teaspoon chili powder.
Curry: Omit dry mustard and 1/2 teaspoon salt and add 1/2 teaspoon curry.
Chervil: Add 2 teaspoons minced.
Chives: Add 1 tablespoon finely chopped.
Chutney: Add 2 tablespoons mango chutney.

Dill seed: Add 1/4 teaspoon.
Fennel: Add 2 teaspoons minced.
Parsley: Add 2 teaspoons minced.
Scallion: Substitute scallion vinegar and add 1 teaspoon minced scallion.

American French Dressing

1 teaspoon egg yolk
2–3 teaspoons Dijon mustard
Dash Tabasco sauce
1/2 teaspoon finely chopped garlic
  or onion
Salt to taste
Ground pepper to taste

1 teaspoon vinegar
1/2 cup olive oil or less depending
  on taste
1 or 2 teaspoons fresh lemon juice
  or more
1 teaspoon heavy cream or more

Beat egg yolk and add 1 teaspoon of it to mixing bowl. Add mustard, Tabasco sauce, finely chopped garlic or onion, salt and freshly ground pepper to taste, and vinegar. Using wire whisk, beat vigorously to blend ingredients. Still beating, gradually add oil. Continue beating vigorously until thickened and well blended. Add fresh lemon juice. Beat in heavy cream. At this point taste the salad dressing and add more of the following as desired: salt, pepper, mustard, or lemon juice. Makes about 3/4 cup, sufficient for 10–12 cups of salad greens.

Vinaigrette Dressing

Try this with Alda Salad, a mix of endive with tomatoes, chopped hard-boiled eggs, artichokes, and pimentos (a favorite garnish in Augusta, Georgia, during the Masters Golf Championship).

3/4 cup walnut oil
1/4 cup sherry vinegar
1/4 cup Dijon mustard
Chopped parsley

Fresh salt and pepper, coarsely
 ground
Dash ground garlic, if desired
Splash fresh lemon juice

Mix in glass jar and shake well. Makes $1\frac{1}{4}$ cup.

Creamy Vinaigrette

Try this with Polonaise Salad, a mix of cold cooked potatoes, carrots, and turnips with fresh cucumbers and diced hard-boiled eggs.

1/4 cup tarragon vinegar	1 teaspoon Dijon mustard
Salt and fresh ground pepper to taste	3/4 cup peanut oil
1/2 teaspoon Aromat (Knorr)	1 tablespoon heavy cream
	1 tablespoon mayonnaise

In mixing bowl, combine vinegar, seasonings, and mustard. Add oil in a stream, whisking all the while until blended and thick. Whisk in cream and mayonnaise until well blended. Makes 1 cup.

Fresh Herb Vinaigrette

This is for those who have an herb garden. If you don't and you want to use dried herbs, cut the amount in half; dried herbs are stronger than fresh. Try with Salad Portugaise, a mix of tomatoes cut in quarters, Spanish onions, beets, and red, yellow, and green peppers.

---

1 cup loosely packed parsley
1 tablespoon fresh basil leaves, cut into fine strips
2 tablespoons snipped fresh chives
1 small garlic clove
6 small shallots
3/4 cup salad oil
1/4 cup water

3 tablespoons raspberry vinegar
$1\frac{1}{2}$ teaspoons Dijon mustard
1 teaspoon sugar
2 teaspoons chopped fresh chervil
2 teaspoons chopped fresh tarragon
1/2 teaspoon salt
Fresh ground pepper to taste

Mince parsley, then set aside with basil and chives. In food processor or blender combine garlic and shallots and finely chop. Add oil, water, vinegar, mustard, and sugar. Then add all the spices. Keeps well in refrigerator. Makes $1\frac{3}{4}$ cups.

Thousand Island Dressing

Try with Neptune Salad, a mix of cold cooked lobster, cold new potatoes, and chopped cooked eggs on a bed of Bibb lettuce.

---

3 eggs
4 cups salad oil
5 hard-boiled eggs, finely diced
1 jar (4 ounces) pimentos, drained
   and diced

1 onion, diced
2 green peppers, diced
1 bottle (12 ounces) chili sauce
1 bottle (14 ounces) catsup
Salt to taste

In food processor or blender beat eggs until light. Without turning off machine, slowly pour in oil in a steady stream. Pour mixture into bowl and fold in remaining ingredients until thoroughly mixed.

Dill Vinaigrette

This is also a good marinade for cooked vegetables.

3/4 cup parsley leaves
1 clove garlic
2 teaspoons fresh dill
2 tablespoons red wine vinegar
1 tablespoon lemon juice
3/4 cup salad oil
1/4 teaspoon brown sugar

1 teaspoon sugar
1 teaspoon granulated bouillon
1 teaspoon salt, optional
1 teaspoon fresh oregano
Dash Tabasco sauce
Fresh ground pepper to taste

In food processor or blender chop parsley and garlic until finely minced. With machine still running, add remaining ingredients (if fresh dill and oregano are not available, use half the amount of dried herbs) and process about 2 to 3 minutes until well blended. Makes 1 pint.

FACTS ABOUT OLIVE OIL

Here are a few items of interest from Linda Stradley's Web site, www.whatscookingamerica.net:

Olive oil is one of the oldest culinary oils. In ancient Athens, the olive was a symbol of the city's prosperity, and its oil was used both in cooking and as fuel for oil-burning lamps. Olive oil has been the cornerstone of the Mediterranean diet for thousands of years.

Legend has it that the first olive tree grew on Adam's tomb. Remember the olive branch the dove brought to Noah, signaling the end of the Flood? Olive trees have a life span of 300 to 400 years. Some grow to be 700 years and older.

Olive oil is made only from green olives. Nearly the entire production of green olives in Italy is converted into olive oil. Flavor, color, and consistency vary, like fine wines, due to different olive varieties, location, and weather. The olive oils of some small producers are treated and priced like fine vintage wines.

Premium Select Extra-Virgin Olive Oil: This is the top grade of olive oil. With a lower rate of acidity than 1%. Some as low as .225%. This level of quality can only be achieved one way—through hand harvesting and pressing within 24 hours.

Extra-Virgin Olive Oil: Any olive oil that is less than 1% acidity, produced by the first pressing of the olive fruit through the col [cold] pressing process. Most olive oils today are extra virgin in name only, meeting only the minimum requirement.

Extra virgin is a chemical requirement that does not indicate quality and taste.

Virgin Olive Oil: It is made from olives that are slightly riper than those used for extra-virgin oil and is produced in exactly the same manner. This oil has a slightly higher level of acidity ($1\frac{1}{2}\%$).

Pure Olive Oil: Also called commercial grade oil. It is solvent-extracted from olive pulp, skins, and pits; then refined. It is lighter in color and blander than virgin olive oil. It is more general-purpose olive oil. Pure refers to the fact that no non-olive oils are mixed in.

Excerpted with permission from www.whatscookingamerica.net.

Chapter 9

ON THE POTOMAC

$\mathcal{W}$hite House social secretary Cathy Fenton spends her days planning some of the most sought-after invitations in the nation's capital. The ongoing progression at 1600 Pennsylvania Avenue includes receptions, garden parties, state dinners, and lavish luncheons. She pores over guest lists and oversees the calligraphy for the invitations, not to mention the entertainment and the seating. She glides through it effortlessly. Now, with First Lady Laura Bush, she's a veteran, after also working on the staff for Barbara Bush and Nancy Reagan.

"My husband would say we don't entertain enough," Cathy says from her office, "which is true." They prefer dinner parties in the spring and summer with grilled fresh salmon or swordfish. "Usually six or eight, a dozen is a lot," she adds.

Is there a difference in Southern salads? "Most decidedly," she says. "There are more nuts and fruit and less cheese. Farther north there are more cheese concoctions."

For a final touch, Cathy likes to add an edible flower, "A nasturtium or a pansy, if available." One would expect nothing but panache from such a graceful lady.

Lorraine Wallace has always entertained effortlessly. It could be a birthday party for the children or a buffet for the Washington, D.C. crowd. Her salads are colossal and tasteful. She and her husband, Chris Wallace (chief correspondent for ABC News *20/20*), "from time to time have a sit down dinner. We prefer small, no more than eight." For this, Lorraine will serve the salad as the third course with greens and cheese. Her basic dressing is simple, one part balsamic vinegar and the rest in extra virgin olive oil. A favorite mix includes baby spinach, sliced pears and avocados, and chopped pecans toasted in butter. "It tastes like bacon," she says.

Champagne Dressing

Perfect for New Year's Eve or a quiet dinner for two. Cathy Fenton likes to use mixed greens, red leaf lettuce, Boston lettuce, and "maybe a bit of radicchio." She often adds pears and "my favorite—toasted chopped pecans."

1/2 cup olive oil
1 tablespoon lemon juice
Salt to taste

Fresh ground pepper to taste
1/2 cup champagne

Make this dressing at the table when serving champagne. Combine oil, lemon juice, salt, and pepper in small bowl and blend well with fork. Pour in champagne and stir briskly to mix. For a tangier dressing, add 1/2 teaspoon Dijon mustard. Serve immediately. Makes 1 cup.

The Naked Truth

In Washington, D.C. all journalists and writers have their "sources." We even have them when we're writing about salad dressings. This recipe comes to me from one of those secret sources, leaked from a very well-known restaurant along the Potomac: "I know this sounds terribly simple," the source says. "It's heavenly, if followed exactly. People beg for it all the time. If only they knew how simple it is! Enjoy."

Begin with greens at room temperature.

Sprinkle generously with extra virgin olive oil.

Toss.

Sprinkle with salt.

Toss.

Sprinkle with balsamic vinegar (1/3 the amount of olive oil).

Toss.

Sprinkle with salt.

Toss.

Serve.

Do not miss a step, do not miss a detail.

And you will end up "Best Dressed."

FACTS ABOUT LETTUCE

"Modern lettuce had its start as a Mediterranean weed. As early as 55 B.C., lettuce was served on the tables of Persian kings and praised for its medicinal values. The name comes from Latin words referring to its milky juice." (www.produceoasis.com)

"Lettuce is one of the oldest known vegetables and is believed to be native to the Mediterranean area. Egyptian tomb paintings suggest that lettuce was cultivated before 4500 B.C."
(www.co.monterey.ca.us/ag/information)

Arugula—Also known as rocket, it was originally from the Mediterranean region. It's said to grow in the wild of southern Europe. At first glance, arugula can appear to look like spinach. It has a strong, piquant, heady essence.

Belgian Endive—Known by the Belgians as "White Gold," this elegant and tangy lettuce has only one calorie per leaf. It was discovered in 1830. Visit www.belgianendive.com, a most amusing site on lettuce, complete with lively music!

Bibb—This soft, tender lettuce was developed by an amateur horticulturist from Kentucky, John Bibb. Also known as Limestone, it was eventually named for him.

Curly Endive—This variety is from the same botanical family as Belgian endive, Cichorium or chicory. Best described as "frilly" with a mild yet tart taste, it's used in Europe as a cooked vegetable.

Iceberg—last but not least iceberg is certainly still very popular, especially "dressed" as a wedge. It's known also as crisphead and should be round and firm.

Lamb's Lettuce—Also known by the French word *mache*, it has a hint of nut flavor.

Mauna—An eye-catching Japanese green with fluffy leaves, this lettuce has a slight piquant flavor.

Radicchio—Italian in origin, it has a dark purplish red color with white ribs. Advise from www.radicchio.com says to "select tight, firm radicchio heads that feel heavy for their size" and "avoid very small heads (less than 1/2 pound)—they're old."

Romaine—A long head of medium green color, no Caesar salad should be made without it. It is also known as "Cos," after the Aegean Island of the same name, where it was reportedly discovered.

Spinach—Popeye's favorite is loaded with antioxidants. First found in Persia, it comes from a botanical family of Chenopodiaceae, or Goosefoot, because the large very dark green leaves are said to bear a similarity to the webbed feet of geese.

INDEX